Next find the *Big Dipper*
in seven stars there.
It's part of a shape
that we call the Great Bear.

I'll bet *Little Dipper*
could scoop up the air!
And sometimes it goes
by the name Little Bear.

Here's *Taurus the Bull*.
Can you see his red eye?
Just look for his face
and his horns in the sky.

Is it *M*? Is it *W*?
Both can be seen.
Who's the star
of the heavens?
Cassiopeia the Queen!

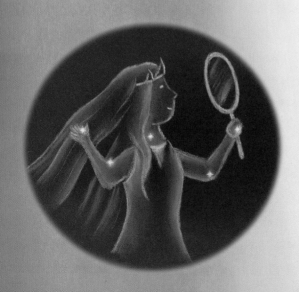

Cygnus the Swan
is a wonderful sight!
To find it just look for
a cross in the night.

A square and a triangle—
Pegasus, of course!
Look! Up in the sky!
It's the flying, winged horse.

There's *Draco the Dragon*!
Just follow his trail.
He prowls in the sky
with his long, curvy tail.

A backward question mark
forms his head.
It's *Leo the Lion*,
with stars for a bed.

Sirius, the Dog Star,
so bright in the sky,
forms part of the *Big Dog*.
Little Dog's nearby.

Three stars for a belt
and a knife shining bright.
It's *Orion the Hunter*,
who hunts in the night!

You're never alone
when the stars
are in view.
Just imagine the world
that is gazing at you!
So keep looking up!
Heaven knows
what you'll see.
The sky tells a story,
and you hold the key.

Leo

Orion

Big Dog